Autism? You mean gener improper environment?

Introduction: The Moment Everything Changed..................... 2
    Chapter 1: The Mercury Timeline..7
    Chapter 2: The LD100 That Wasn't......................................10
    Chapter 3: Why Autism Now?...12
    Chapter 4: Mercury Doesn't Just Sit There........................ 15
    Chapter 5: The Autism Machine..18
    Chapter 6: The Blame Loop That Keeps Us Sick................21
    Chapter 7: The Label Trap... 26
    Chapter 8: First, Do Less Harm..31
    Chapter 9: Support the Drain... 34
    Chapter 10: The Nutrient Cycle..40
    Chapter 11: Reading the Reactions..................................... 49
    Chapter 12: Why This Gets Suppressed..............................54
    Chapter 13: The Bigger Picture..60
    Chapter 14: What Now?.. 67
Epilogue: A Note to Parents... 73

Introduction: The Moment Everything Changed

My wife turned off the light as she walked through the room. But this time, I felt it. Not just noticed it, felt it. It sent something through the core of my being, a sensation that wasn't unfamiliar but had never hit at this severity before.

Then the washing machine two rooms away stopped its cycle. The sudden silence triggered an overwhelming feeling of complete hopelessness. I didn't realize it, but that mechanical hum had been holding my world together, and when it stopped, I had nothing. The sun went behind a cloud and I almost broke in two. The hair on my neck stood up like a drill sergeant had just walked in the room, except it wasn't just the hair on my neck. It was my entire being responding to invisible shifts in my environment.

What is going on? Why am I living and breathing emotions as if everything is wired together and short circuiting?

I had poisoned myself with iodine. And it ended up being one of the best mistakes I ever made. It led me on a journey that finally helped me understand life. Over the next few years I went from being overwhelmingly confused by the world to understanding it better than most. Decades of trying to figure out how to handle the world turned into the exact training I needed to stand up to it, regain my health, and share one of the most unique experiences a human can have.

Let me back up.

Other than some common health issues when I was young, which I'll touch on later, I was lucky enough to not have any major problems that required attention. Life was manageable. But in my mid-thirties I fell for a flu shot and everything changed. Over the next six months I started noticing general fatigue, anxiety, panic, brain fog, confusion, tingling fingers, rapid heart rate, headaches, terrible sleep. Name it, I started feeling it.

It was all setting in slowly, worrying me more each week, but what could I do? Go to a doctor I didn't have and say "hey, I feel really weird"? Run a billion tests and get prescribed drugs for symptoms nobody could explain?

Then everything changed again. It took a few times to realize what was happening, but I was waking up on the floor having seizures. And my health was deteriorating with each one.

As I tried to figure out what in the world was going on, I looked at my dog Kiwi. She used to be a great puppy, and then for some reason she slowly turned into a terror. Chewing everything, peeing everywhere, barking, growling, not listening. We blamed ourselves for not training her right. But then it clicked.

It's the injections. I was fine, and now I'm waking up on the floor short circuiting. Kiwi was fine, and now she's a "bad dog." Same timeline. Same trigger.

I'm not saying Kiwi and I were at one hundred percent before all this, that these injections magically gave us autism or turned us into completely different beings. But the pattern was there once I knew to look for it. This is part of how I'm able to understand what I'm sharing with you in this book. A little bit more about me and then we'll get started.

My first memory is being reprimanded for taking apart my Christmas toy with a screwdriver I wasn't supposed to have while unattended. Since then I've been on a mission to figure out how just about anything works. I have this strange sort of OCD where if I want to understand something, I cannot stop thinking about it until I have a complete picture in my head. Not just surface level. I need to understand the mechanism.

I built my first computer when I was about ten. The internet didn't exist yet, which made learning significantly harder. Later I installed large networks in schools, put together a satellite array on a Navy building, built large websites and business systems. I wouldn't have graduated high school if it weren't for hacking the school computers and changing my grades. I didn't pay attention in class, but I could teach myself anything I was interested in. The problem was that school wasn't teaching things I found interesting or useful.

I struggled my whole life because I could see how things work, but I didn't realize I was part of a world where almost everything is inverted. Truth gets called misinformation. Poison gets called medicine. Sickness gets called normal. Although my health crash was extremely inconvenient, it led me to iodine, which finally helped me see things for what they actually are.

Starting iodine helped the seizures right away. Almost immediately I felt my brain coming back online. But then I assumed I needed to continue pushing into more and more iodine because that's what the iodine communities constantly push. I didn't fully agree with the idea of ramping up to huge doses, but it's hard to figure out what to do when the only guidance the community gives is "take more."

Over the course of about three months, I slowly made my way up to about thirty-five milligrams of almost daily iodine. That's when the weird symptoms started creeping back. What do I do now? I'm taking a good bit of this weird brown liquid that tastes like I imagine coins would taste, a handful of other nutrients to support it, and I'm starting to feel like I'm going to crash again.

I tried adding B vitamins. I tried focusing on electrolytes. Nothing worked. The only other option I knew of at the time was pushing into even more iodine. I didn't agree with the approach but it was one of the few options the community talked about. Looking back I realize I was just taking too much iodine too quickly. First I satisfied an iodine deficiency, which gave my cells enough energy to pull me away from seizures. But then I pushed hard enough to mobilize toxins, which increased the burden on my already maxed-out system.

I pretty quickly doubled my iodine intake, trying doses around one hundred milligrams for a few days. I didn't feel any better. Actually seemed to slowly feel worse. So I stopped. Three days later I woke up feeling like I'd been hit by a bus. My whole body hurt. I could barely get out of bed. Even my feet hurt, which was bizarre.

I woke up to my boss calling. After essentially crawling across the house to call him back, I realized I could barely form sentences. I couldn't think straight, I could barely speak, and as I continued to wake up, panic set in. What in the world is happening to me?

All I could do was lay on the couch in full panic mode, my heart feeling like it was going to explode out of my chest. It's hard to describe just how bad these days were. The worst I've ever felt, and I've been through some things. This went on for days. And this is where I felt emotions in ways I never imagined possible, which finally allowed me to realize I'm on the spectrum.

After about a week of this, with symptoms slowly getting better, I ate a handful of deviled eggs one night. The next morning I woke up feeling eighty percent better.

That's when I started researching. Sulfur in the eggs. Mercury binding. The detox pathway I'd accidentally triggered and then cleared. And then the flashbacks started coming: my mom laughing, her mouth full of dark amalgam fillings. Both grandmothers, same thing. Mercury, passed down through generations, tucked into my cells before I was even born.

I finally understood what I was.

The label came later. Autism, high-functioning, whatever they want to call it. But the label didn't matter. What mattered was understanding the mechanism. The biochemistry. The reason why I'd spent my entire childhood in bathroom stalls crying from gut pain nobody could explain. Why I was called a "retard" at parties until I started drinking, and then suddenly became the life of the party. Why I could see patterns others couldn't, but couldn't figure out how to express basic emotions.

My brain wasn't broken. My metabolism was jammed.

And once I understood that, I could finally start unjamming it.

This book is what I wish someone had told me thirty years ago. It's what I wish someone had told my mom, and her mom. It's the map I had to draw myself because nobody else would admit the territory even existed.

If you're reading this, you probably already know something isn't right. Maybe it's your kid. Maybe it's you. Maybe you've been searching for answers and all you get is "it's genetic" or "it's a mystery" or "learn to cope."

This isn't a mystery. This is biochemistry. And once we understand what's actually happening, we can do something about it.

Chapter 1: The Mercury Timeline

Here's what they don't want us to connect. In the 1830s, amalgam dental fillings were introduced in the United States. Within years, dentists started reporting that their patients were experiencing tremors, emotional instability, and kidney problems. The response? The American Society of Dental Surgeons required members to sign pledges not to use amalgam. The pledge didn't hold. Too profitable.

By the 1840s and 50s, "Mad Hatter Disease" was recognized. Hat makers working with mercury to cure felt developed tremors, mood swings, hallucinations, and cognitive decline. Everyone knew mercury caused this. It wasn't a secret. But it didn't stop anything.

Through the late 1800s, mercury was used widely in medicine as a laxative, a diuretic, and a treatment for syphilis. It was known to be toxic, but "the dose makes the poison," they said. Meanwhile, amalgam fillings became standard practice despite all those early warnings.

The 1930s brought thimerosal, ethylmercury developed and added to vaccines as a preservative. Declared safe and effective. Then came the post-WWII industrial boom of the 1940s through 60s, with mercury in pesticides, fungicides, and industrial processes. Into the soil, into the water, into the fish, into us.

The 1970s saw lead finally phased out of gasoline after decades of known harm. Big victory for public health, they said. Meanwhile, mercury use continued elsewhere, quietly. Through the 80s and 90s, autism diagnosis rates started climbing. One in ten thousand. Then one in a thousand. Then one in five hundred.

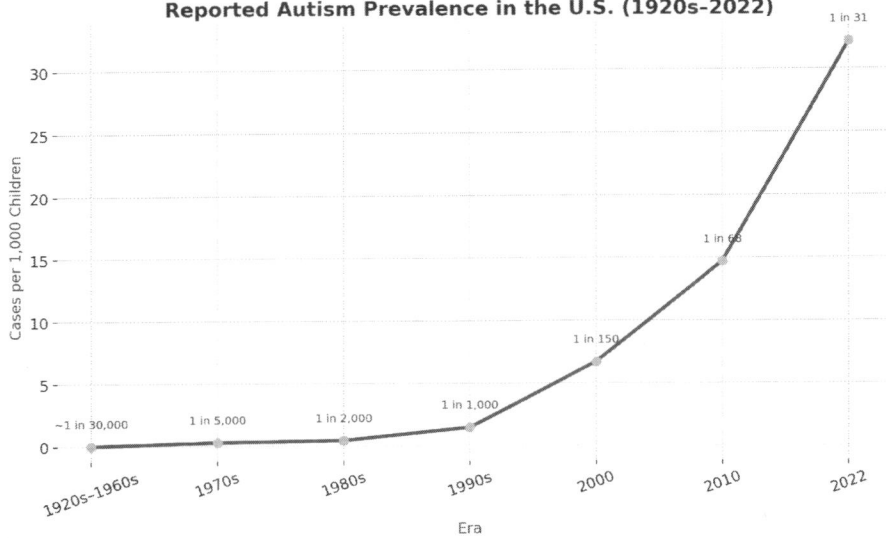

By the 2000s, some countries started phasing out amalgam fillings. Not because they admitted they were wrong, just because "newer materials are available." No apology. No acknowledgment. Just quietly moving on. And now in the 2020s, autism rates have hit one in thirty-six children. Still climbing.

Every single time, the same thing happens. They introduce a mercury-containing product. Immediate reports of harm come in. They defend it for decades. Then they quietly phase it out. They never admit why. They just move on to the next thing.

They knew amalgam fillings were causing problems in the 1830s. They knew industrial mercury was poisoning hat makers. They knew lead was poisoning children for fifty years before they removed it from gasoline. They always know. They just don't care enough to stop until the liability becomes too obvious.

And here's what they're not connecting: autism rates didn't explode randomly. They exploded in the generations born to parents and grandparents who had mercury tucked into their teeth, breathing mercury-laden air, eating mercury-contaminated fish, getting mercury-preserved vaccines. This is generational accumulation. Each generation starts with more burden. Each generation breaks down faster. Each generation has less metabolic reserve to handle additional improper environment.

We're not dealing with a genetic mutation that spontaneously appeared. We're dealing with the compounding effects of industrial poisoning that nobody wants to admit happened.

Are you under the impression mercury toxicity is random?

From pathwaymap.com/mercury-exposure "The evidence overwhelmingly demonstrates that mercury exposure has become an inescapable aspect of modern existence. From the 2,220 tonnes released annually by human activities to the 890,000 kilograms liberated by wildfires, mercury saturates our environment at every level. With 92.9% of Americans showing detectable mercury and similar rates worldwide, the concept of "mercury-free" living is a practical impossibility. "

Chapter 2: The LD100 That Wasn't

Here's a study that should have changed everything. Researchers gave mice what they called LD100 doses of mercury. LD100 means "lethal dose one hundred percent," the amount that kills every single subject. Except only ten percent of the mice died.

Why? The mice had alcohol in their system.

Somehow, alcohol protected ninety percent of them from a dose that should have killed them all. The mercury was still there, but something about the alcohol temporarily counteracted its effects.

Now let me tell you about high school. I was the weird kid. Couldn't connect with people, couldn't express myself, struggled to understand social cues. At parties, people called me a "retard." Not behind my back, to my face. And honestly, I couldn't even argue. I felt broken.

Then I started drinking at these parties. Suddenly, I was the life of the party. Funny, engaging, able to connect with people. The anxiety melted away. The constant pressure in my head eased. I could finally feel somewhat normal.

And here's the weird part: I stopped getting sick. All through childhood, I was sick constantly. Every year, multiple times a year. Gut issues that had me crying in bathroom stalls. Mysterious symptoms nobody could explain. But once I started drinking regularly? It stopped.

I thought I'd just "grown out of it." Now I know what actually happened. The alcohol was temporarily mobilizing mercury. Just like those mice, I had a lifelong mercury burden I didn't know about. The alcohol wasn't making me "fun," it was temporarily relieving mercury toxicity. My real personality could finally come through when the poison wasn't actively jamming my neurotransmitters.

This raises a massive question. How many people are walking around with subclinical mercury poisoning, self-medicating without knowing why? How many people "need" coffee to function? "Need" alcohol to relax? "Need" weed to calm anxiety? "Need" stimulants to focus?

What if a huge percentage of our coping mechanisms are just accidentally counteracting heavy metal toxicity? What if the reason those substances "work" for some people and not others has nothing to do with genetics or personality, and everything to do with toxic load?

If alcohol can protect mice from LD100 mercury doses, if alcohol temporarily relieved my autism symptoms, if this is reproducible and observable, then how many people are living with heavy metal burdens that are just below the threshold of obvious poisoning?

And here's the darker question. Is this happening on purpose? Not the poisoning itself, necessarily. But the cycle. Poison the population. Watch them develop symptoms. Offer substances, legal and illegal, that temporarily relieve those symptoms. Create dependency. Profit from both the poisoning and the "solutions."

I can't prove intentionality. But I can see the pattern. And the pattern is too consistent to ignore.

Chapter 3: Why Autism Now?

Let's be clear about something. Autism as we know it today is not an ancient condition that we're just "recognizing better now." Yes, there have always been people who struggled socially, who thought differently, who had sensory sensitivities. But one in thirty-six children is not better recognition. That's a systemic collapse.

Something changed. And it changed fast.

The first generation, born in the 1930s and 40s, saw widespread amalgam fillings becoming standard, industrial mercury exposure ramping up, and the first generation with mercury-preserved vaccines from birth. The chemical revolution was beginning with pesticides and industrial solvents everywhere.

The second generation, born in the 1950s through 70s, came into the world already carrying mercury from parents who had it in their teeth, blood, and tissues. They inherited mercury burden through the placenta, then added their own exposure through more vaccines, more industrial chemicals, and increasingly nutrient-depleted soil. This is when we started seeing the early labels: "hyperactive," "learning disabled," "behaviorally disturbed."

The third generation, the 1980s through 2000s, was born to parents who were already compromised. Two generations of accumulated metals, nutrient-depleted food becoming standard, plastics and fire retardants and pesticides everywhere. Autism rates started climbing noticeably. One in five hundred, then one in two hundred and fifty.

Now we're in the fourth generation, the 2000s to present. Born to parents carrying three generations of toxic burden with minimal metabolic reserve left. One additional stressor and the system buckles. One in thirty-six and climbing.

This isn't genetics. This is generational poisoning. Genes don't change that fast. But epigenetics, the switches that turn genes on and off, those get jammed by toxins. And those jammed switches get passed down. Each generation starts weaker. Each generation needs less additional stress to break. Each generation has less ability to detox what comes in.

The drain was already clogged. We just keep pouring more down it.

And here's what makes autism specifically: it's not just generic toxicity. It's toxins that specifically target neurological function. Mercury has an affinity for fat and sulfur. Our brain is sixty percent fat. Our detox pathways run on sulfur. Mercury jams both.

So brain development is altered because the fat-based structure is compromised. Neurotransmitter production gets jammed because sulfur pathways are blocked. Detox systems are paralyzed because they can't clear what's coming in. The system is forced to adapt in increasingly dysfunctional ways. That adaptation is what we call autism.

But why doesn't everyone have autism if this is true? Because it's a threshold effect. Some people have better baseline genetics with stronger detox enzymes. Some inherited less burden because their parents had less exposure. Some have better nutrition compensating for some damage. Some face fewer additional stressors like infections, mold, EMF, or chronic stress.

People forget that our "genes" are just factories which are made of the nutrients we consume. When our bloodline has been swimming in toxicity, stressing, or somehow avoiding nutrition, our "genes" are weak factories doing whatever they can to attempt getting through the wrong environment without all the stuff they need.

They're still accumulating damage. They're just not past their breaking point yet. But look around. Anxiety, depression, ADHD, autoimmune conditions, chronic fatigue, gut issues, all exploding alongside autism. We're all dealing with the same problem. Autism is just what it looks like when multiple systems break at once in a developing brain.

The spectrum isn't a mysterious variation or genetic disorder. It's the spectrum of how much toxic burden each person is carrying and how well their system can still compensate.

Each generation has a different type of autistic. HIgh-functioning boomers are usually successful. They haven't been hit with enough toxicity alongside mercury. I was born in 1981 and I have a mix of intelligence and anger. I was an angry kid and I did a lot of stupid things and almost ended up in jail. Generations after me are mainly just jacked up. The autism/adhd groups are loaded with people that can't start a lawn mower, but they can quickly tell me nutrition couldn't possibly have anything to do with the way we behave. Then you get a few odd ones from clean bloodlines that are still able to focus and use the "gift'.

Chapter 4: Mercury Doesn't Just Sit There

Let's talk about what mercury actually does in the body, because this is where the mechanism becomes clear. Mercury binds to sulfur. Specifically, it binds to sulfhydryl groups, the thiols, the sulfur-containing parts of proteins and enzymes. And here's the problem: sulfur chemistry is central to almost everything your body does.

When mercury binds to these sulfur groups, it jams glutathione production and function. Glutathione is your master antioxidant and detoxifier. It's a sulfur-based compound. Mercury blocks it directly. Now you can't detox anything else either.

Mercury also jams metallothionein proteins. These are the proteins that bind and neutralize heavy metals. They're sulfur-rich. Mercury blocks them, so now other metals like copper, cadmium, and lead start accumulating too.I consider mercury the Gate Keeper.

The entire sulfur metabolism pathway gets disrupted. The transsulfuration pathway that makes glutathione, the methylation cycle that makes neurotransmitters and DNA and everything else, both depend on sulfur chemistry. Both get blocked by mercury.

Hundreds of enzymes throughout our body have sulfur-containing active sites. Mercury binds to them and inactivates them. Metabolic pathways grind to a halt.

Once glutathione is depleted, our body has a backup plan: burn fat differently. Normally, fat metabolism runs through proper pathways, gets broken down efficiently, and produces energy cleanly. But when glutathione is gone and mercury is jamming the system, the body switches to emergency metabolism.

This is where autism symptoms emerge. Fat isn't being processed properly, so brain structure is affected since the brain is sixty percent fat. Energy production shifts and everything goes straight into high-rev metabolism. We can't gain weight because everything is being burned inefficiently immediately. And there is no leftover fat to wrap toxins in fat, so they just go right through metabolism. We can't calm down because we're stuck in high-rev mode. Brain pressure increases as metabolic waste backs up. Neurotransmitters can't be made properly because methylation is jammed. They can't be broken down properly because detox is jammed. They recycle endlessly, leading to emotional dysregulation, sensory overload, and anxiety.

This isn't theoretical. This is documented biochemistry. The only debate is whether it's happening on purpose.

Mercury also destroys beneficial gut bacteria. Lactobacillus, Bifidobacterium, the good guys that help us digest food, make vitamins, and regulate immunity, mercury kills them preferentially. What survives? Yeast. Candida loves mercury. It actually uses mercury as a tool to compete with other organisms. Mercury strengthens the bad guys while wiping out some of the good. Remember all that "our guy feeds our brain" stuff?

So now we have gut bacteria decimated, yeast overgrowing and producing acetaldehyde, a toxic metabolite. Acetaldehyde crosses into the bloodstream and affects the brain, causing fog, rage, and depression. Leaky gut develops as the gut lining gets damaged. Undigested food particles escape into the blood, triggering immune reactions. Food sensitivities appear out of nowhere. Mmm, more 'sensitivities', exactly what we need (sarcasm).

Things like Candida are likely nature's response to nutritional/toxic energy that is not being used properly. It's very likely helping us buffer this stuff.

The gut issues aren't separate from the brain issues. They're the same mercury-driven cascade. This is why autistic kids so often have chronic constipation or diarrhea, food sensitivities, and "picky eating" which is actually an inability to digest certain foods. Their behavior changes based on what they eat because their gut can't process food. The unprocessed food feeds yeast. The yeast produces toxins. The toxins affect the brain. The brain symptoms get labeled "autism."

Another huge issue here is sometimes we find a substance, good or bad, that moves mercury. The mercury tries to get out, but it can't, which is part of the reason it's still here anyway. Our poor gut, already damaged, is bombarded with more mercury. Now our gut takes on more damage, and guess where the mercury goes? Not out, again.

Fix the gut, support detox, and the "autism" often improves dramatically.

But.. we're not supposed to notice that.

Chapter 5: The Autism Machine

Let's walk through exactly how a jammed metabolism expresses as autism. Step by step. This isn't mysterious.

Mercury and other metals accumulate, inherited from generations of mothers through fillings and exposures, added through the environment via food, vaccines, air, and water. The system can't detox them efficiently because it's already compromised, so they store in **fat tissue**, including the brain. Hmm, where does it go if our **fat metabolism** has been destroyed? Directly into our autism?

Glutathione production fails because mercury blocks the enzymes that make it. Now you can't detox anything. Toxic load increases exponentially. Oxidative stress skyrockets.

Fat metabolism switches to emergency mode. Without glutathione, the body can't process fats properly. Everything burns fast and dirty. You can eat massive amounts without gaining weight. Constant high-rev metabolism means constant stress-state.

Methylation pathways jam up. You can't make neurotransmitters properly. You can't break them down properly. Serotonin, dopamine, norepinephrine, all dysregulated. Either too much or too little, never balanced.

"Why are you such an emotional wreck?"

Because neurotransmitters can't be broken down, they get recycled. The same stress signal fires over and over. The brain gets stuck in loops. Anxiety, obsessive thoughts, emotional dysregulation all emerge from this recycling. But, what else are you running through the machine all day? Petro colors? Mold?

High oxalate foods with poor oxalate metabolism due to poor fat metabolism?

Sensory processing breaks down. Neural signals aren't being filtered properly. Everything comes in too loud, too bright, too intense. The nervous system can't distinguish signal from noise. Constant overwhelm becomes the baseline.

Think about how this would play out. Instead of having the right amount of "feelers" out on something, we have 1,000x as many, and these feelers are half corrupted and don't fire properly. Imagine any machine trying to run with an excess of half broken sensors.. No wonder Walmart used to make me feel like I was at an amusement park.

Brain pressure builds as **metabolic waste** products can't be cleared. Inflammation increases. There's physical pressure in the head. Sometimes it's so intense that speech becomes impossible. This isn't good.. pathogens enjoy **metabolic waste**..

The system tries to adapt. Shutdowns happen when you can't process any more input. Meltdowns occur as attempts to discharge overwhelm. Stimming is an attempt to regulate through repetitive input. Rigidity develops as a way to reduce variables because the system can't handle change. Just receiving verbal input is enough to overwhelm the system.

This is autism. Not a mysterious genetic condition. Not a "different way of being." A system under siege, adapting in the only ways it can to keep functioning.

The difference between "high-functioning" and "low-functioning" comes down to how many pathways are jammed, how severe each blockage is, how much reserve capacity remains, and how much additional stress is present. Someone called high-functioning might have a moderate mercury load that's not overwhelming, some methylation still working, decent gut health compensating, and learned coping strategies that work well enough. Someone called low-functioning might have a severe toxic burden across multiple metals, complete methylation failure, destroyed gut with constant inflammation, no reserve capacity left, and every day is survival mode.

Some people with more toxins grow up with less stress and more love. Others grow up with various levels of stress and don't know what love is.

Some of us are born to bloodlines carrying a lot of toxicity, others are hit with things just before and after birth, and some are hit with both

Same mechanism. Different magnitudes. And here's the thing: high-functioning people can crash into low-functioning territory with enough additional stress. It's not a fixed category. It's a measure of how close to the edge we're operating. I found my edge.

I've had periods where I couldn't speak because the pressure in my head was so intense. I've had times where I lashed out at people because I couldn't process what I was feeling. I've broken things and harmed myself in the process, out of frustration. I've been on that edge. The difference between me writing this book and someone who can't function isn't fundamental. It's just how many rocks are currently in our gears.

Remove enough rocks, and function improves. Add more stress, and function declines. It's a dynamic system, not a permanent state. But we aren't paying attention to how our environment works and our cells are tapping out.

Chapter 6: The Blame Loop That Keeps Us Sick

Here's something we need to understand before we can heal anything. None of us chose this. Your mom didn't choose to pass mercury to you. Her mom didn't choose it either. They were doing their best with amalgam fillings in their mouths, drinking fluoridated water, eating from aluminum cans, breathing leaded gas fumes. You didn't choose to struggle. Your kid didn't choose to have meltdowns. Your partner didn't choose to be emotionally unavailable.

We're all operating under the influence of toxic load. Our behaviors, our emotional reactions, our inability to connect, these aren't character flaws. They're jammed metabolism expressing itself as jammed thinking and jammed feelings.

When we hold onto resentment toward our parents for "giving us this," guilt for "passing it to our children," anger at partners who "just don't get it," or shame for our own struggles and failures, that stress itself keeps the drain clogged.

Emotional stress uses up glutathione. Glutathione uses up… everything. Unresolved resentment keeps cortisol elevated. Shame keeps us in fight-or-flight. All of this makes detox impossible. We can't heal while we're blaming. And we can't stop blaming until we understand: everyone is a victim of the same poisoned system.

Our mom yelling at us for behaviors we couldn't control? She had mercury altering her neurotransmitters too. She was doing her best with a broken operating system. Our meltdowns as a kid? Not a moral failure. Our metabolism couldn't process what we were feeling. The pressure in our head was real, physical, biochemical. The weird kid at school who couldn't fit in? That was our nervous system running on the wrong fuel, trying to navigate a world while our perception was scrambled.

None of it was our fault. Or their fault. Or anyone's fault at the individual level.

With autism, with more mercury, more metabolic rocks, more jammed pathways, our emotions are more confusing, our perceptions are more distorted, our reactions are more extreme, and the world makes less sense. And then people tell us we're "gifted" or "special" or we "just need to try harder." What tf are you even talking about? Try harder at what? Not understanding anything?

Our mind is tweaked by "rocks" in our metabolism. Remove the rocks by rebuilding the system, and our mind isn't as tweaked. The world makes more sense. It's not that reality changes. It's that we can finally process reality without everything running through a chemical funhouse mirror.

There's a forgiveness protocol that's as important as the detox protocol. First, forgive the system. We're living in the aftermath of industrial poisoning that nobody acknowledged. Multiple generations have been damaged. This happened. We can be angry about it, but we have to let go of that anger to heal.

Second, forgive the people. Everyone in your life, parents, siblings, kids, partners, they're all running on jammed systems too. Even the people who "seem fine" are just earlier in the process or compensating in ways we don't see. Their hurtful behaviors weren't about you. They were about their own jammed metabolism expressing as jammed emotions.

Third, forgive yourself. Every meltdown, every failure to connect, every time you lashed out or shut down or couldn't explain what you felt, you were doing your best with a system that wasn't working properly. You're not broken. You're not defective. You're not "less than." You're a human trying to function with rocks in your gears. And now you're learning how to remove the rocks. And now you also have experiences that can help others see what we're going for, just like someone has likely for you.

Fourth, extend this understanding forward. When your kid has a meltdown, it's not willful, it's a jammed system. When your partner doesn't understand, it's not uncaring, it's different toxic load and different perception. When someone dismisses your experience, it's not malicious usually, they just can't see what they haven't felt.

When we stop holding grudges against people who are just as much victims as we are, something shifts. The chronic stress response calms down a little. The resentment that was burning energy constantly releases. The shame that was keeping us in fight-or-flight dissolves. And suddenly we have more energy for actual healing.

This is why life seems so difficult, especially with autism. We're trying to navigate relationships and society and emotions while our mind is being altered by metabolic dysfunction. Of course nothing makes sense. Of course we feel lost. But as we rebuild the system and remove the rocks, our perception clears. We can finally see that other people weren't intentionally cruel, they were just struggling too. We weren't intentionally difficult, we were literally unable to process what was happening.

When you're working through detox and old emotions start surfacing, don't re-traumatize yourself by re-blaming. "My mom shouldn't have yelled at me," she had mercury too, let it go. "I should have been a better parent," you were doing your best with jammed gears, let it go. "They should have understood," they couldn't feel what you felt, let it go.

Feel the emotion as it surfaces. Acknowledge it. Then release it with understanding: everyone was doing their best under the influence of poison.

This doesn't mean accepting ongoing harm. If someone in your life is still toxic because they're still heavily loaded and refusing to address it, you can have compassion and boundaries. "I understand you're struggling with your own system, and I can't let that drain mine anymore." Forgiveness doesn't mean staying in the blast radius. It means not carrying the resentment after you step away.

Holding onto blame and resentment is like trying to detox while drinking from a poisoned well. You can take all the right supplements, eat all the right foods, get all the sunlight, but if you're still running your nervous system on stress from unresolved anger, you're fighting yourself.

The physical detox and the emotional release have to happen together. As the mercury leaves, old emotions surface. As we process those emotions with forgiveness instead of blame, more mercury can leave. It's a spiral. Either downward where we hold onto everything, or upward where we release as we go.

Choose the upward spiral.

When our metabolism is jammed, our thinking is literally altered. Not just our emotions, our actual logic. Decision-making requires neurotransmitters. Pattern recognition requires clear neural signaling. Emotional regulation requires balanced brain chemistry. Social understanding requires proper gut-brain communication. When all of these are compromised by toxic load, we develop coping mechanisms based on faulty data.

"People are scary, better avoid them." Reality: our nervous system was in constant fight-or-flight from metabolic stress. Our brain interpreted this as external threat. Social isolation became our "solution." But it was just a bandaid to the problem.

"I have to be perfect or I'm worthless." Reality: our system couldn't handle stress, so any additional pressure felt catastrophic. Our brain interpreted this as "I must prevent all mistakes." Perfectionism became our "solution." But it just added more stress.

We built entire belief systems on top of biochemical malfunction. And now, as we detox, we get to rebuild those belief systems with clearer data. People aren't inherently threatening, my nervous system was just maxed out. I don't need to be perfect, I just need to support my system so normal stress doesn't feel catastrophic. The world isn't impossible to navigate, my perception was scrambled.

As the rocks come out, notice which beliefs start feeling less true. Don't force it, just observe. New understanding will naturally emerge. Life will literally make more sense. This is why people often report "finally feeling human" when they detox properly. It's not that they're becoming someone new. They're finally thinking clearly for the first time. The world was always there. They just couldn't see it clearly through the chemical fog.

Chapter 7: The Label Trap

Here's a problem. We're using one word, "autism," to describe what's actually multiple different metabolic breakdowns happening in various combinations. It's like calling everything that makes our car run poorly "engine disorder" when actually it could be bad fuel, clogged air filter, worn spark plugs, low oil, broken timing belt, or any combination of these. Each one needs different support. But we're treating them all the same because they produce similar symptoms.

When we look at what's actually happening biochemically, "autism" is usually some combination of mercury and heavy metal toxicity jamming sulfur metabolism, glutathione and detox pathways, undermethylation where you can't produce neurotransmitters properly and can't turn off stress response, overmethylation where you're overproducing some neurotransmitters leading to anxiety and sensory overload, pyrrole disorder dumping zinc and B6 causing emotional volatility and poor stress tolerance, copper toxicity often alongside undermethylation creating emotional blunting or extreme emotions, histamine issues either too high with allergies and anxiety or too low with low motivation and high pain tolerance, fat metabolism failure where you can't process fats properly affecting brain structure and hormone production, and gut dysfunction with microbiome dysbiosis and leaky gut feeding into all the above.

Each of these has sub-categories and overlaps. Someone might have heavy metal toxicity plus undermethylation plus pyrrole disorder. Someone else might have overmethylation plus histamine issues plus gut dysfunction. Both get called "autism." Both need completely different support.

This is why some kids respond dramatically to certain interventions and others don't. We're not all dealing with the same thing. The current approach is "You have autism, here's behavioral therapy." A better approach would be "Let's figure out which metabolic pathways are jammed and support those specifically." If it's undermethylation, you can likely make use of small amounts of methyl donors, support SAMe, and specific B vitamins. If it's pyrrole disorder, zinc and B6 levels are likely destroyed. If it's copper toxicity, zinc is likely needed to push copper out, plus support emotional processing. If it's heavy metals, we need to build up glutathione and support detox pathways.

One-size-fits-all doesn't work because there isn't one thing happening.

And here's the second part, this is important. You don't need an official autism diagnosis to benefit from this information. If you read this book and think "*holy poop, that's me,*" that's enough. If you relate to feeling overwhelmed by everything, difficulty expressing emotions or not feeling them at all, sensory sensitivities, gut issues that doctors can't figure out, brain fog and difficulty focusing, social situations feeling impossible, meltdowns or rage that seem disproportionate, or feeling like you're broken or on a different wavelength, you don't need permission from a professional to address your metabolism.

Labels serve two purposes. One is insurance and access, getting services, accommodations, and disability support. Sometimes you need the official diagnosis for this. Two is understanding and community, finding people who get it, making sense of your experience, knowing you're not alone. But here's what labels don't do. They don't tell you what's actually wrong biochemically. They don't tell you what support you specifically need. They don't change who you are.

You're not "an autistic person." You're a person with specific metabolic issues which produce specific symptoms. And once you understand those specific issues, you can address them, diagnosis or not.

Modern culture wants us to identify with our labels. "I'm autistic" as identity. "I'm ADHD" as identity. "I'm anxious" as identity. This serves the system because identity means permanent means lifelong customer. If it's "who you are," you don't try to change it. You accept management instead of pursuing resolution.

But we're not our dysfunctions. We're humans with jammed systems trying to function. As we unjam the systems, the dysfunctions reduce. That's not "masking" or "betraying our identity." That's literally fixing what was broken.

If you have a diagnosis, great, now dig deeper. Which specific metabolic issues are at play for you? What actually needs support? If you don't have a diagnosis, but relate, start addressing the underlying issues anyway. You don't need permission. If you're a parent of a diagnosed kid, the label might help you access services, but don't let it limit your understanding of what's actually happening. Your kid isn't "autistic" as a fixed state. They have specific biochemical roadblocks that can be addressed. If you're not sure where you fit, it doesn't matter. If these metabolic issues resonate, address them. You'll know pretty quickly if they're relevant based on how you feel.

Yes, there's a spectrum. But it's not a mysterious spectrum of "autism severity." It's a spectrum of how many metabolic pathways are jammed, how severe each jam is, how much reserve capacity we started with, and how much additional stress we're under. Someone with mild symptoms might have moderate heavy metal load, decent methylation still working, one or two pathways struggling, and good gut health compensating.

Someone with severe symptoms might have heavy metal toxicity across the board, multiple methylation issues, all pathways compromised, destroyed gut microbiome, and depleted nutrient reserves.

Some people live near high voltage power lines, have every wifi product available, a cellphone in their pocket or within a foot or two 24/7, wireless earbuds, moldy homes, work, or cars, live with stressful people, live downwind of air toxicity, drink toxic water, and on and on.

Same fundamental problems. Different degrees of magnitude. This is why "spectrum" language is misleading. It implies a mysterious gradient of one condition. Really it's different combinations and severities of multiple metabolic breakdowns.

Your experience is valid without a label. If you struggled your whole life without knowing why, finally read something that makes it all click, realize your symptoms match metabolic dysfunction, or start addressing it and feel better, you didn't need a diagnosis. You needed understanding. The label is just shorthand. What matters is recognizing what's actually wrong, addressing the root causes, supporting your specific needs, and connecting with others who get it. You can do all of that without ever setting foot in a diagnostic office.

This doesn't mean ignore medical professionals, work with good ones when you can. We're not saying reject all labels, they can be useful tools. We're not saying go it completely alone, community matters. We're saying don't let labels limit your understanding. Don't tie your identity to dysfunction. Don't wait for permission to address obvious metabolic issues. Don't accept "mysterious disorder" when there are clear biochemical explanations. If relating to these experiences is enough to start helping yourself, that's enough.

Some parents worry about whether they should get their kid diagnosed. Consider whether they need accommodations at school, which might require a diagnosis for an IEP. Consider whether they're getting harmed by people not understanding, which might need a diagnosis for protection. But if you just want to understand and help them, you don't need a diagnosis. Just start supporting their system. Many kids have improved dramatically without ever getting an official label. The biochemistry doesn't care about paperwork.

We're not trying to collect labels, build identity around dysfunction, justify ourselves to others, or get validation from the system. We're trying to understand what's actually wrong, fix what can be fixed, support what needs ongoing support, and live better lives. Labels are tools. Use them when helpful. Ignore them when they're not.

Your experience is valid. Your struggles are real. Your path to healing doesn't require anyone's permission. If this book resonates with you, if you see yourself in these patterns, that's all you need to start making changes. The label "autism" was never going to fix anything anyway. Understanding your specific metabolic issues and addressing them, that's what actually helps.

Chapter 8: First, Do Less Harm

Before we start adding things, we need to stop doing harm. The system is already maxed out. If we keep pouring poison down a clogged drain while trying to unclog it, we're fighting ourselves.

Let's start with fish because there's nuance here. We don't want to avoid fish entirely. We want to choose wisely. Smaller fish lower on the food chain accumulate less mercury. Sardines, anchovies, wild salmon, these are generally safe and incredibly nutrient-dense. Bigger predator fish like tuna, swordfish, and shark accumulate more mercury because they eat smaller fish and concentrate the toxins.

But even high-mercury fish might sometimes be worth it for the omega-3s, vitamin D, selenium, and complete protein package they provide. The calculation matters. If you're eating salmon twice a week, the selenium and other nutrients help protect against and mobilize the small mercury load. If you're eating tuna every day, you're losing that math. Context matters. A nutrient-depleted person eating tuna occasionally might come out ahead. Use your judgment. We're trying to shift the balance, not achieve perfection.

Pay attention. If adding fish lights up our brain in a good way and calms us down, it's probably good. But if it causes issues with sleep and vision or anything weird like that, it's probably not working out right now.

Now let's talk about stopping new mercury exposure. No new amalgam fillings, obviously. If you have existing fillings, don't rush to remove them. Improper removal can dump massive amounts of mercury into your system all at once. If you do remove them, find a dentist trained in safe removal protocols with proper suction, rubber dam isolation, and immediate supplementation support. Everyone in the room should look like they are going to space. Otherwise everything in that office is likely covered in mercury.

Watch out for other sources. Some vaccines still contain thimerosal, particularly flu shots and some given in developing countries. Some nasal sprays, contact lens solutions, and cosmetics contain mercury compounds. Check labels. Reduce what you can.

The other metals matter too. Aluminum in cookware, foil, antiperspirants, some antacids and buffered medications. Lead in old paint, old pipes, some imported ceramics and cookware. Cadmium from cigarettes and plastic products. These all add to the total toxic burden and many of them interact synergistically with mercury to make everything worse.

Seed oils are wrecking our fat metabolism. Soybean oil, canola oil, corn oil, vegetable oil, all the polyunsaturated omega-6 fats that are in everything processed. When our fat metabolism is already jammed from mercury, these oils pour gasoline on the fire. They oxidize easily, create inflammation, and interfere with proper omega-3 utilization. Switch to butter, ghee, tallow, coconut oil, olive oil. Real fats that your body knows how to process.

Oxalates need to be reduced, but slowly. Oxalates are compounds in many plant foods that can cause problems, especially when gut health is compromised and we can't break them down properly. They bind to minerals, create crystals, cause pain and inflammation. High-oxalate foods include spinach, almonds, chocolate, sweet potatoes, beets. But here's the catch: if we suddenly cut oxalates, our body starts dumping stored oxalates. This can cause severe symptoms, the "oxalate dumping" phenomenon. So reduce them gradually over months, not days. And understand this isn't primarily an oxalate problem.

It's a fat metabolism problem. Once fat metabolism improves, oxalate handling usually improves too.

Water filtration matters. Fluoride in tap water is another halogen that competes with iodine and jams thyroid function. Chlorine kills gut bacteria. Heavy metals leach from old pipes. Get a good filter. Spring water or a distiller if you can afford it, at minimum a carbon filter that removes chlorine and some other contaminants. This is one of the highest-leverage investments you can make.

Electromagnetic fields are a wildcard. Some people are more sensitive than others, but when our nervous system is already maxed out from toxic load, EMF can be the straw that breaks the camel's back. Keep phones away from your body. Turn off WiFi at night. Don't sleep next to your phone or electrical panel. Get morning sunlight while grounded to help set circadian rhythm and protect against EMF damage. We're not saying become paranoid, but reduce unnecessary exposure where it's easy.

Plastics are everywhere and they're wrecking hormones. BPA, phthalates, all the endocrine disruptors leaching from bottles, containers, packaging. Don't microwave in plastic. Don't microwave anything. Don't leave plastic water bottles in hot cars. Switch to glass or stainless steel where you can. Every bit helps when the system is already struggling.

Stress is using up our glutathione and keeping us in fight-or-flight. This is biochemical, not just psychological. Chronic stress depletes the very nutrients we need for detox. We'll talk more about the forgiveness piece and letting go of resentment, but understand that managing stress is not optional if you want to heal. It's as important as any supplement.

The goal isn't perfection. The goal is reducing the incoming load enough that your system can start catching up. Every small change adds up. You're not trying to live in a bubble. You're trying to shift the balance from "constantly overwhelmed" to "manageable" so healing can actually begin.

Chapter 9: Support the Drain

Now that we've stopped pouring as much poison in, we need to get the drain working again. This is foundational. If the drain is clogged, nothing else we do will work properly. We'll just be pushing toxins around inside a backed-up system.

Sunlight is primary fuel. This isn't hippie nonsense, this is biochemistry. When light hits our skin, it doesn't just make vitamin D. It sets off a cascade of hormonal and metabolic processes that regulate everything else. Morning sunlight, the red and infrared wavelengths, sets our circadian rhythm. This rhythm controls when our body detoxes, when it repairs, when it produces hormones, when it rests. Without proper light exposure, this entire system drifts out of sync.

Autistic physiology tends to tank indoors under LEDs and screens. We've noticed this if we've paid attention. Kids who are bouncing off the walls inside will often calm down outside. It's not just "getting energy out." It's the nervous system finally getting the input it needs to regulate properly. The light is literally feeding our mitochondria. Red and near-infrared wavelengths penetrate tissue and help mitochondria produce energy more efficiently. When our mitochondria are already struggling from toxic load, this support becomes critical.

Get outside in the morning, as early as we can. Even ten or fifteen minutes. No sunglasses, let the light hit our eyes. This tells our brain it's daytime, sets cortisol properly, prepares melatonin for later. Throughout the day, get as much natural light as possible. If we're stuck inside, be near windows. The difference between indoor artificial light and natural light through a window is significant. Red light therapy devices can supplement, especially in winter, and we don't need expensive LED panels.Wear blue blockers when artificial light dominates natural sunlight. I wear them 100% of the time when its dark outside, and I wear them less as I'm able to get out into the sun every 20 minutes or so.

Real food means nutrient-dense, not calorie-dense. Our bodies are starving for nutrients while drowning in calories. Every processed food is stealing from us. It takes nutrients to process and digest food. When the food doesn't contain enough nutrients to cover its own processing cost, we go into deficit.

What does nutrient-dense mean? Animal foods first. Meat, especially organ meats if we can handle them. Eggs, particularly the yolks. Fish and shellfish. Bone broth. These foods contain nutrients in forms our bodies can actually use, with all the cofactors needed for absorption. They contain complete proteins with all the amino acids we need to rebuild tissue and make neurotransmitters. They contain fat-soluble vitamins A, D, E, and K that are critical for hormone production, immune function, and brain health.

Then vegetables, but cooked and with fat. More than a small amount of raw vegetables are hard to digest when our system is compromised. Cooking breaks down cell walls and makes nutrients more accessible. Adding fat, butter or ghee or tallow, helps us absorb the fat-soluble vitamins and makes the food more satiating. We're not trying to be rabbits. We're trying to rebuild a broken system.

Fruit in moderation. Yes, it has vitamins and minerals. But it also has sugar, and when our metabolism is already dysregulated, too much sugar just feeds yeast and spikes blood sugar. A few berries, sure. A whole fruit smoothie, probably not helpful right now. Most fruit is saturated with pesticides which can load us with toxic copper or other similar compounds that do not show up till for a while.

Fermented foods can be powerful, but we need to start slow. Sauerkraut, kimchi, kefir, yogurt if we tolerate dairy. These contain beneficial bacteria and help rebuild gut microbiome. But if we're heavily loaded with yeast, fermented foods might make things worse at first. Start with a teaspoon and see how we respond. We can always add more later.

Bile flow is critical and almost nobody talks about this. Bile is our body's dish soap. The liver makes it, the gallbladder stores it, and we release it when we eat fat to help break down and absorb that fat. But when bile flow is sluggish, fat backs up. Undigested fat feeds the wrong gut bacteria. Fat-soluble vitamins don't get absorbed. Toxins that the liver packaged into bile to be eliminated get reabsorbed back into our bloodstream. We're literally recycling our own poison.

Signs of poor bile flow include pale or floating stools, constipation, inability to digest fatty foods, nausea after eating fat, and gallbladder pain or removal. Many autistic kids have some or all of these signs. Their parents learn to avoid fatty foods because it causes problems. But avoiding fat just makes the underlying issue worse because we need fat for brain function and hormone production.

How do we support bile flow? Bitter foods. Arugula, dandelion greens, endive, radicchio, coffee if we tolerate it. Bitters signal the liver and gallbladder to release bile. Apple cider vinegar in water before meals. Lemon juice. These acidic foods help stimulate digestion. Digestive enzymes with ox bile can help if we need more direct support. These aren't forever, just while we're rebuilding. But they can make a massive difference in how we feel and how well we absorb nutrients.

Gut lining rebuilding happens when we remove irritants and provide building materials. The irritants we already talked about: seed oils, excess sugar, processed foods, anything we're sensitive to. The building materials are glycine, glutamine, zinc, and vitamin A. Bone broth is the easiest way to get glycine and some of the other amino acids needed. Collagen or gelatin powder works too. These provide the raw materials to repair the intestinal lining. Most of these are great for initial repair or topping off at times, but I don't supplement any of them regularly.

Zinc and vitamin A work together. Vitamin A from animal sources, liver being the best source or cod liver oil if we can't handle liver. Zinc from meat, shellfish especially oysters if we can get them, or supplemental zinc. These two nutrients are critical for tight junction integrity, the connections between our gut cells that keep undigested food from leaking into our bloodstream.

Most do not realize vitamin A is doing something crazy with sunlight. So it's not always vit A itself that's the problem. Lack of bile and sulfite metabolism push vit A out of the cell which is another problem. Vit A is a hormone and likely needs more precaution and education. Supplementing a little once in a while is likely fine, but pushing it whether it feels better or not likely isn't going to work out like we assume.

When we talk about leaky gut, we're talking about those tight junctions being compromised. Undigested food proteins escape.

Our immune system sees them as foreign invaders. Creates antibodies against them. Now we have food sensitivities that weren't there before. This creates inflammation throughout our body, including in our brain. Brain inflammation shows up as brain fog, mood swings, rage, anxiety, the whole spectrum of neurological symptoms.

As we heal the gut lining, many of these sensitivities resolve. Not all of them, and not immediately. But over months of consistent support, we often find we can reintroduce foods that used to cause problems. The gut heals when we stop irritating it and give it what it needs to rebuild.

Hydration matters more than we think. Not just drinking water, but actually getting water into our cells. This requires minerals, particularly sodium and potassium. If we're drinking tons of water but still feeling dehydrated, we're probably flushing minerals and not replacing them. Good quality salt, real sea salt with trace minerals, not processed table salt. Potassium from foods like potatoes, squash, avocados, meat. These minerals help water actually get into cells instead of just passing through.

When our cells are dehydrated, everything works worse. Enzymatic reactions slow down. Toxin elimination slows down. Nutrient delivery slows down. Simply staying properly hydrated with adequate minerals can improve energy, mental clarity, and stress tolerance significantly.

We need to try more sources of water too even if we're using 'the best'. Sometimes I drink bottled water from Walmart or something weird because someone offers, and it feels like the first time I've had water in 3 days. When this happens I try to stick with that water till the benefits level off and then I cycle through sources again. I do this same thing with just about anything.

Sleep gives our cells time to detox. Our glymphatic system, the brain's waste removal system, works primarily during deep sleep. If we're not sleeping well, we're not clearing metabolic waste from our brain. This waste accumulates, creates more brain fog and pressure, makes everything harder the next day. Supporting sleep means supporting our entire detox system.

How do we support sleep? Consistent schedule, going to bed and waking at the same time. Morning sunlight to set circadian rhythm. Avoiding blue light in the evening, using blue blockers or turning off screens early. Keeping the bedroom cool and dark. Magnesium before bed can help. Sometimes glycine or theanine. If sleep is severely disrupted, we might need to address cortisol dysregulation, but start with the basics. Often fixing other things in the system, particularly nutrient deficiencies and toxic load, will improve sleep naturally.

We don't want to eat after dark or drink coffee or anything stimulating. We're supposed to be calming down and reflecting on the day and preparing for tomorrow. Instead we're stimulating ourselves like crazy with food, light and an endless list by now.

This foundation of sunlight, real food, bile flow, gut healing, hydration, and sleep is not optional. This is the drain. If the drain isn't working, nothing else we add will help. We'll just be pushing toxins around in circles. But when we get the drain working, even a little bit, everything else starts working better. Nutrients get absorbed. Toxins start leaving. Energy improves. Brain fog lifts. The system finally has a chance to catch up.

We're not trying to do all of this perfectly tomorrow. We're trying to move in the right direction, consistently, over weeks and months. Every small improvement compounds. The body wants to heal. We just need to remove the obstacles and provide support. Get the drain unclogged, and the rest becomes possible.

Chapter 10: The Nutrient Cycle

Now we're getting into the layers. This is the onion. Each layer we peel reveals the next one underneath. Each layer will kick up stuff. We need to let it clear before going deeper. If we rush this, we'll make ourselves worse. If we pace it right, we'll systematically rebuild the system from the ground up.

This is not "take these supplements and feel better." This is "support these specific pathways in this specific order because each one depends on the one before it." When we understand why we're doing what we're doing, we can adjust based on how we respond. We become our own best guide.

Start with magnesium because every cell in our body needs it and most of us are depleted. Magnesium is involved in over three hundred enzymatic reactions. Energy production, protein synthesis, muscle relaxation, nerve transmission, blood sugar control, blood pressure regulation. When we're stressed, and being full of toxins is a form of stress, we burn through magnesium fast. When we're low on magnesium, everything else is limited. We need magnesium but we likely can't use much right now. So we want to provide some without just dosing ourselves.

Signs of magnesium deficiency include muscle cramps, twitches, restless legs, anxiety, insomnia, constipation, irregular heartbeat, and chocolate cravings. Sound familiar? Most autistic people have several of these. We're not magnesium deficient because we have autism. We're showing autistic symptoms partly because we're magnesium deficient and can't run our nervous system properly. I have this weird disconnected feeling where I don't want to deal with anything at all when I'm low on magnesium. I had this feeling on and off my whole life but especially as my health crashed. I use 100mg of magnesium a day on average and sometimes I go weeks or months without any. But then I notice the familiar feelings creep up and realize I need to get some again.

What kind of magnesium? Different forms do different things. Magnesium glycinate is calming, good for sleep and anxiety, gentle on the gut. Magnesium citrate is more laxative, good if we're constipated but might be too much if we're not. Citrate might be an issue if we're clogged up with mold. Magnesium malate is energizing, good for daytime use. Magnesium threonate crosses the blood-brain barrier, specifically helpful for brain fog and cognitive issues but expensive. We might need to experiment to find what works for us. Many people do well with glycinate at night and malate during the day.

How much? This is individual. Start low, maybe two hundred milligrams, and work up. Some people need six hundred or more. The limit is bowel tolerance. If we get loose stools, we've gone too high. Back off a bit. Topical magnesium, sprays or baths, can also help and don't affect the gut. We're looking for muscle tension to decrease, sleep to improve, anxiety to ease. These are signs our magnesium status is improving.

But once we load up on this a bit, slow down and find the amount you seem to need. We can eventually go toxic in magnesium which most people do not talk about. This is why I stick with 100mg. I seem to have weak kidneys, but something tells me this isn't exactly uncommon. I've had a few people reach out over the years in crisis, which we eventually figure out is due to magnesium overdose.

Potassium works with magnesium. They're the dynamic duo of cellular function. We need both for proper nerve firing, muscle contraction, heart rhythm, and cellular energy production. Most people get some potassium from food, especially if eating real food like we discussed. Meat, potatoes, squash, avocados, bananas. But if we're depleted, food alone might not be enough at first.

Supplemental potassium is trickier because high doses can offset us if its not balanced in some way. I use reputable electrolyte powders with potassium and possibly some magnesium and sodium. Signs we need more potassium include weakness, fatigue, muscle cramps, irregular heartbeat, and strong salt cravings. As our magnesium and potassium come up together, we'll often notice improved energy and stress tolerance.

Now B vitamins, but carefully. This is where methylation comes in. The methylation cycle is how we make neurotransmitters, process hormones, build DNA, and run detox. When methylation is working, we feel stable, focused, energetic. When it's not, we get depression, anxiety, brain fog, poor stress tolerance. Mercury jams methylation directly and inhibits demand for more by breaking systems downstream. So do nutrient deficiencies. We need B vitamins to run the cycle, particularly B12, folate, B6, and B2.

But here's the catch. Some people are undermethylated and need methyl donors. Others are overmethylated and get worse with methyl donors. How do we know which we are? Undermethylated people tend toward depression, obsessive thoughts, perfectionism, seasonal allergies, sparse body hair, strong-willed personality. They often feel better with B vitamins like hydro/adeno B12 and folinic acid. Overmethylated people tend toward anxiety, panic, artistic or musical ability, heavy body hair, self-motivated, sometimes paranoid thinking. They often feel worse with methyl donors and better with niacin which helps move methyl groups down the line.

Methylation is a system that generates energy. Some of us are ready for more energy, but low on the ability to generate more, others are not able to use more energy, but have plenty ready to go. The problem with methylation is sometimes we can't handle more of it, but at the same time we require more of it in order to keep up on the processes needed for life to continue. So part of the system is demanding more while other parts are saying woah, woah, slow down, we can't handle more of what this is causing.

If we needed to burn something indoors to remain warm, we can only get more heat if the air in the room is still breathable. Once the air is maxed with toxicity, we can no longer generate any heat till the air is resolved. Methylation cannot generate more energy when toxicity is maxed.

B6 deserves special mention because it's critical for neurotransmitter synthesis and many autistic people are severely depleted, often from pyrrole disorder. Pyrroles are metabolic byproducts that grab onto B6 and zinc and drag them out of the body. If we have pyrrole disorder, we're constantly losing these nutrients no matter how much we eat. Signs include morning nausea, poor dream recall, white spots on nails, stretch marks, poor stress tolerance, and emotional volatility. Many autistic people test high for pyrroles. Supporting this requires higher doses of B6, usually the P5P form which is active, and zinc. But again, start low and work up. Too much B6 can cause nerve issues over time, though the active form is safer.

Some people go toxic with B6 very quickly, and this likely has to do with issues in our sulfur line. But I think autism and related situations have low B6 because the whole sulfur line has been in high demand any time any related nutrients have been available. What I mean is our sulfur line is always trying to operate, and anytime any nutrients are around at high enough levels and allow that to happen, b6 is used. I think this is happening because whatever is causing autism seems to be using the sulfur line whereas most other situations are not putting as much pressure on sulfur directly. If those toxins did push on sulfur, they would likely push further into autism symptoms.

Sulfur metabolism is huge for autism. Remember mercury jams sulfur pathways. Glutathione is sulfur-based. When we can't make or use glutathione, we can't detox. Supporting sulfur metabolism means we start being able to clear toxins. But this needs to happen slowly because as toxins start moving, we'll feel it.

Sulfur-rich foods include eggs, the best source and easiest to digest. Cruciferous vegetables like broccoli, cauliflower, cabbage, but cooked. Garlic and onions. Meat, especially organ meats. If we've been low on sulfur for a long time, adding these foods back in might cause reactions. We might feel worse before we feel better. This is mobilization. Start with small amounts. Half an egg. A few bites of broccoli. Work up slowly over weeks. If something backfires, don't be discouraged, be a detective. You now have an important clue.

I think one of the best things we can do if we have the money is buy liposomal glutathione that either contains these nutrients or is taken after we provide small amounts of: molybdenum, selenium, b2 and PQQ. We don't need or want much liquid liposomal glutathione, but tiny amounts might help us start lifting a heavy burden on our system, or have a better idea where we're bound up. Proper glutathione function is an end goal, but part of the reason for that is due to glutathione functioning properly as our whole system is able to function properly. So properly glutathione means proper metabolism.

Some people do well with NAC, N-acetyl cysteine, which is a sulfur-containing amino acid that helps make and stimulate glutathione. Start very low, maybe one to three hundred milligrams, see how we feel. If we get irritable, anxious, or develop brain fog, we're mobilizing too much too fast. Back off. If we feel better, clearer, more energy, we're supporting detox without overwhelming it. This is the balance we're looking for. NAC can be great, but it seems to force glutathione, which is not great if glutathione cannot function properly atm. Just pay attention to pros or cons of adding this.

Glycine is another piece of the glutathione puzzle. Glutathione is made from three amino acids: cysteine which we get from sulfur, glutamine, and glycine. Many people are limited by glycine. It's the smallest amino acid, easy to absorb, and has calming effects on the nervous system. Bone broth, gelatin, collagen all provide glycine. Or we can supplement with glycine powder, it's cheap and effective. A few grams before bed can improve sleep and support detox at the same time.

But, glycine is an important compound of bile, and bile isn't able to function properly at the moment. As we move forward we will have better bile function, but for now, the lack of proper bile is going to inhibit glycine's ability to balance properly. This means too much glycine can mean too much bile even though we might see glycine boosting glutathione in a good way. This is a good example of the mysteries we'll run into with nutritional balancing. It might seem overwhelming and up in the air, but it's not much different than a gasoline engine backfiring. That backfire is alarming at first but once we investigate, we're able to understand why it's happening.

Selenium is critical when working with sulfur because it protects against the mobilization of mercury and helps convert it to forms that can actually leave the body. Brazil nuts are thought to be high in selenium, but they tend to be moldy and that's not something we want to consume regularly. I use a 200mcg selenomethionine supplement once per week while keeping an eye out for symptoms of high or low selenium. I list these at whyiodine.com/selenium. Selenium is a very important nutrient but some of us are not able to use it yet.

Selenium helped me see how to handle nutrients. I felt nothing from it at first. But then after making progress with other nutrients over time, I tried some again and went from feeling like complete crap, to feeling much better. This helped me realize there are times I can take an important nutrient and not feel anything, and then there are times it can be a game changer. Over time I realized this is because I'm slowly providing my cells with whatever it is they need in order to move forward, and eventually they get to the point there they can handle more nutrients in order to carry out more things.

Which brings up iodine.

Eventually we get to iodine, and this is where things can get intense. Iodine displaces bromide, fluoride, and eventually mercury and anything else in our tissues via apoptosis. This is good because we want these things out. But if we displace too much too fast without adequate support systems in place, we'll feel terrible. This is what happened to me with the couch incident. I took too much iodine too fast without understanding I needed to support things like electrolytes, bile, stomach acid, sulfur metabolism and glutathione first.

The approach is low and slow. One drop of Lugol's two percent solution is about two and a half milligrams of iodine. Start with that, or even half a drop, or use nascent or other weak iodine if you tend to react to things. Take it near selenium and vitamin C. See how it feels. If brain fog increases, if we get more anxious or emotional, if old symptoms flare up, we're mobilizing faster than we can clear. Back off, support the other systems more, try again in a few weeks. If we feel more energetic, clearer, warmer especially in hands and feet which suggests better thyroid function, we can slowly increase. Very slowly. We might stay at one drop for months before going to two. This is not a race.

Some people need higher doses eventually, twelve to fifty milligrams for therapeutic detox and even more to push things out sometimes. But we only get there after months or years of building up slowly with all the support systems in place. Iodine can be incredibly powerful for clearing out the garbage, but it's also powerful enough to hurt us if we're not ready for it.

Think of a massive project that is much more work than you can handle at the moment. And think of diving into that project when there is obviously not enough time to tackle it. This is an obvious issue when we think of an overwhelming project. But when it comes to cellular detox and healing, we don't see it.

We only want as much iodine as we have time and energy to clean up the mess of. We want to clean the windows but we don't want to spray a ton of cleaner only to realize we don't have the energy or rags to finish cleaning up the mess before it oozes onto the wall.

The pattern here is: each nutrient supports the next level. Magnesium allows potassium to work. Both allow B vitamins to work. B vitamins allow methylation to work. Methylation and sulfur metabolism work together to make glutathione. Glutathione allows us to handle iodine mobilizing deeper toxins. Now metallothionine can function better and start carrying copper which can carry iron which can support molybdenum to convert sulfites to sulfates while helping generate bile. It's a cascade. If we try to jump to iodine without the foundation, we'll crash. If we build the foundation first, iodine can be the key that unlocks deep healing. We need tiny amounts of iodine at first to help get our cells moving in the right direction. Over time they will help us employ more cells which can use more iodine.

This takes time. Months to years. But we're not only throwing supplements at symptoms. We're systematically rebuilding the metabolic machinery that was jammed by toxins. As each system comes back online, the next one becomes possible. This is how we actually fix what's broken instead of just managing symptoms forever.

Chapter 11: Reading the Reactions

Learning to read what our body is telling us is might be the most important skill in this whole process. We're all different. What works for someone else might not work for us. What dosage is perfect for one person might be too much or too little for another. We need to become expert observers of our own responses.

When we add something new and feel worse, there are a few possibilities. First, we might be mobilizing toxins faster than we can clear them. This is the most common cause of negative reactions. The supplement is doing what it's supposed to do, moving junk out of storage, but our exit pathways aren't keeping up. The solution is not to push through. The solution is to back off, support the exit routes more, bile flow, hydration, maybe some activated charcoal or bentonite clay to bind toxins in the gut, or just more unrefined salt and more water, and try again slower later.

Second, we might be feeding something we don't want to feed. If we're trying a new probiotic and we feel worse, we might be feeding yeast instead of good bacteria. If we're trying B vitamins and getting more anxious, we might be overmethylated and pushing the cycle the wrong direction. The solution here is to stop that particular thing and try a different approach, or just give things more time.

Third, we might be having an actual allergic or sensitivity reaction. This is less common but possible. If we break out in a rash, develop breathing issues, or have immediate digestive distress, that's our body saying no to this particular form of this nutrient. Try a different brand or form, or just skip that particular supplement and get it from food instead. If the reaction was not intense, a good way to see what's going on is to reduce the dose to 10% or less and try again in a few days to a week. If we never seem to react better, it's likely our cells saying no way.

When we add something new and feel better, that's usually straightforward. We were deficient, now we're less deficient and our system is working better. Stay at that dose for a while. Let the system stabilize. Don't immediately increase thinking more is better. Sometimes more is just more. Sometimes less is actually the right amount long-term and we only needed more temporarily to fill the tank.

We run into an issue with a few nutrients like methyls and vitamin D or starting at high doses with anything. This is a confusing one at first but these things are bypassing all the stuff I'm talking about. This is like ignoring a worn out car in need of maintenance, and instead finding some sort of mega-fuel-5000 to get it running better. A good sign is when "you just need this one thing", and once someone highlights some of the issues with isolated nutrients, it turns into "oh, you just need these two things, err three things". Everyone is trying to juice our system to force it to feel better. That's not how long term health works, it's how we got here in the first place.

The tricky reactions are the mixed ones. We feel better in some ways and worse in others. More energy but also more anxiety. Better focus but worse sleep. This usually means we're on the right track but need to adjust dose or timing or add support for a related pathway. If magnesium is giving us energy but making us too wired at night, we're probably taking too much or the wrong form or we need it earlier in the day. If iodine is clearing brain fog but increasing anxiety, we probably need more sulfur support to handle what the iodine is mobilizing.

Emotional reactions are important information. If old emotions start surfacing, especially emotions we don't remember feeling before, that's stored toxins moving. Mercury affects the limbic system, our emotional processing center. As it leaves, we might re-experience emotions that were happening when it originally got stored. This can be intense and confusing. We might suddenly feel rage about something from childhood. We might cry for no apparent reason. We might feel anxious about things that logically we know aren't threatening.

This is not "the supplement is making us crazy." This is "the toxins that were making us crazy are finally leaving and we're processing what was frozen in place." The key is not to re-traumatize ourselves by attaching stories to these feelings. Just feel them, acknowledge them, let them move through, remember that everyone was doing their best under the influence of poison, and let them go. If we can do this, these emotional releases actually clear stuck energy and we feel lighter afterward.

Physical detox symptoms can include headaches, usually from toxins being mobilized, skin breakouts as toxins exit through the skin, changes in bowel movements either constipation as the body holds onto toxins it can't process or diarrhea as it tries to flush them fast, muscle aches especially in areas where we've held tension, and fatigue as the body diverts energy to detox. None of these are fun, but they're all signs that things are moving. The question is always: are we moving things faster than we can clear them, or is this manageable discomfort on the way to better function?

If symptoms are mild and we can still function, probably okay to continue. If symptoms are severe or lasting more than a few days, we've pushed too hard. Back off, increase support for elimination, let things calm down. There's no prize for suffering through this. Slow and steady wins this race.

Plateaus are normal and actually necessary. We'll have periods where we're improving steadily, then periods where nothing seems to be changing. This is often the body consolidating gains, rebuilding at a deeper level, preparing for the next phase. Don't panic and start adding a bunch of new things. Just hold steady. Keep supporting the basics. The next breakthrough will come when the system is ready. We might be waiting for our brain to let go of a broken mindset now that we have clearer logic circuits.

Sometimes we'll have setbacks. Stress, illness, exposure to toxins we couldn't avoid, poor sleep, whatever. We'll feel like we're back where we started. This is discouraging but temporary. We haven't lost all our progress. The system is just overloaded temporarily. Go back to basics, increase support, be patient with ourselves. Function will return once the acute stressor passes, and often we'll bounce back to a higher baseline than before because the underlying foundation is stronger.

Try to find a silver-lining in everything. For example, if a glass falls and breaks, instead of getting mad, I try to think about what happened so I can attempt to avoid it in the future. Getting mad doesn't do anything but get me worked up and more depleted.

Kids present special challenges because they can't always articulate what they're feeling. We're reading behavior changes. If our kid is sleeping better, having fewer meltdowns, making more eye contact, showing more interest in connecting, those are all positive signs even if nothing dramatic is happening yet. If our kid suddenly regresses, gets more aggressive, stops sleeping, those are signs something isn't working. Either we're moving too fast, or we accidentally introduced something they're reacting to, or there's an unrelated stressor like illness or changes at school.

The key with kids is patience and observation. Change one thing at a time. Wait at least a week or two to see the effect. Keep a simple log if we need to, nothing fancy, just date and what we changed and general observations. Over time patterns will emerge. We'll learn what helps and what doesn't for our specific kid.

We're not looking for perfect compliance or perfect reactions. We're looking for general trends in the right direction over weeks and months. Two steps forward, one step back is still progress. One step forward, maintaining, then another step forward is excellent progress. We're rebuilding systems that took years or generations to break. This doesn't happen overnight.

Trust the process. Trust observations. Trust that our body wants to heal and will tell us what it needs if we learn to listen. The mainstream medical system largely ignores this whole approach, so we're not going to get validation from doctors for most of this. That's okay. We're getting validation from how we feel, how our kids are improving, how life is becoming more manageable. That's the only validation that matters.

Chapter 12: Why This Gets Suppressed

Let's talk about why nobody wants us to connect these dots. It's not always a conspiracy in the shadowy-figures-in-rooms sense, though that might exist too. Mostly it's simpler and more insidious: incentive structures.

Follow the money. Always follow the money. When a truth threatens multiple billion-dollar industries simultaneously, that truth doesn't get told. Not because there's a meeting where villains decide to suppress it. Because everyone operating within those systems has reasons not to look too closely.

The dental industry would collapse if amalgam liability was admitted. Imagine the lawsuits. Dentists have been installing mercury in people's mouths for almost two hundred years while claiming it's safe. If they admitted it wasn't safe, if they acknowledged the generational damage, the liability would be astronomical. Easier to phase it out quietly, claim "newer materials are available," and never admit fault. Move on. Hope nobody notices.

The pharmaceutical industry is built on symptom management, not root cause resolution. If autism is actually heavy metal toxicity and nutritional deficiency, then the solution is nutrients, not lifelong behavioral therapy and psychiatric medications. An autistic person on our current system might be a customer for life. Medications for anxiety, depression, sleep, seizures, behavioral issues. Therapies, specialists, interventions. We're talking hundreds of thousands of dollars per person over a lifetime. If the root cause gets fixed, that revenue stream disappears.

This isn't evil necessarily. It's just how systems optimize. Pharmaceutical companies are legally obligated to maximize shareholder value. A cure that costs a few hundred dollars in supplements is bad for business compared to lifelong medication management. Nobody needs to be actively malicious. The system just naturally suppresses information that threatens profitability.

The medical establishment is stuck in institutional inertia. Medical school doesn't teach nutrition beyond a few weeks of basics. It doesn't teach functional medicine or systems thinking. It teaches diagnose, prescribe, manage symptoms. Doctors come out of medical school with massive debt and limited tools. When we show up with a kid showing autistic symptoms, they have a protocol. Diagnose, refer to behavioral therapy, maybe prescribe something if symptoms warrant it. That's what they know how to do.

If we start talking about mercury detox and methylation support, we're speaking a language they weren't taught. And because they weren't taught it, they assume it's not real or not valid. Their worldview doesn't have room for it. This is cognitive dissonance, not malice. But the effect is the same: dismissal, mockery, being told to stop looking at dangerous misinformation on the internet.

The regulatory agencies are captured by the industries they're supposed to regulate. The FDA, the CDC, they're staffed by people who came from pharmaceutical companies and will likely return to pharmaceutical companies. This is called the revolving door and it's well documented. When the people making regulations have financial ties to the companies being regulated, those regulations tend to favor industry over public health.

Nobody needs to explicitly bribe anyone. The bias is built into the structure. An FDA official who's too hard on pharmaceutical companies won't get hired back into industry after their government stint. So they learn to be reasonable, to compromise, to accept industry data at face value. And if that industry data says thimerosal is safe, well, they don't dig too deep. Career preservation becomes more important than truth-seeking.

The media is funded by pharmaceutical advertising. Flip on any news channel and count the drug commercials. Billions of dollars flow from pharmaceutical companies to media companies every year. This creates a chilling effect. Media companies are less likely to run stories that are critical of their biggest advertisers. Journalists learn not to bite the hand that feeds them. Stories about pharmaceutical harm get less coverage. Stories about natural approaches get dismissed as woo-woo. The information ecosystem gets shaped by who pays for it.

Academic research is funded by the industries being researched. Most autism research is funded by pharmaceutical companies or by organizations with pharmaceutical ties. These funding sources determine what questions get asked and what questions don't. Research that might implicate vaccines or medications doesn't get funded. Research looking at genetic markers or brain differences gets plenty of funding because it doesn't threaten anyone's bottom line. The questions we ask determine the answers we find. If we never ask "could this be heavy metal toxicity," we'll never fund studies that might prove it.

Independent researchers who do look at these connections get marginalized. They lose funding. They get labeled as quacks or anti-vaxxers. Their papers get rejected from journals. Not always through explicit censorship, though sometimes. More often through social pressure and professional consequences. Academia is hierarchical and reputation-driven. Go against the consensus and watch opportunities dry up. Most researchers learn to stay in their lane.

Parent communities get infiltrated and redirected. Online forums about autism recovery get flooded with people telling parents not to try biomedical interventions, that it's dangerous, that autism isn't something to be cured. Some of these people genuinely believe what they're saying, bought into the "neurodiversity" framing. Others might have other motivations. It's impossible to know. But the effect is that parents trying to help their kids get discouraged, shamed, told they're harming their children by attempting detox or dietary changes.

The neurodiversity movement, while having some valid points about acceptance and accommodation, serves to reinforce the idea that autism is an identity rather than an injury. If autism is just a different way of being, then looking for causes or cures is offensive. This framing benefits the system because it stops people from asking uncomfortable questions about what caused the autism explosion. We're told to celebrate differences instead of investigating origins. Again, some people promoting this genuinely believe it. But the outcome is that investigation gets labeled as harmful.

Legal liability creates powerful motivation for suppression. If environmental toxins and medical interventions caused a generation of brain alterations, the lawsuits would bankrupt multiple industries. Amalgam manufacturers, vaccine manufacturers, chemical companies, anyone involved in the mercury supply chain. The legal exposure is incomprehensible. So there's enormous pressure to ensure that causation never gets officially established. Settle individual cases quietly if needed. But never admit systemic causation.

About a fifth of all gold has likely used mercury to help separate it from sediment. I think this is a good way to see how much money involved with mercury.

Government agencies can't admit past mistakes because it would undermine public trust. If the CDC admitted that vaccine preservatives contributed to autism, people would stop trusting vaccines entirely. If the FDA admitted that amalgam fillings were poisoning people for generations, people would stop trusting the FDA. So they're trapped. Admitting error would cause more immediate harm than continuing the cover-up. From their perspective, they're choosing the lesser evil. Protect the system, protect public trust, and hope better solutions can be implemented quietly over time.

This is why we see things get phased out without explanation. Thimerosal mostly removed from childhood vaccines, but never an admission it was harmful. Amalgam fillings quietly discouraged in some countries, but no official acknowledgment of past harm. Lead removed from gasoline after fifty years of damage, framed as a proactive environmental improvement rather than an admission of mass poisoning. The pattern repeats. Quietly fix the problem, never admit there was a problem, hope people forget.

Insurance companies don't want to pay for nutritional interventions. They'll pay for behavioral therapy because it's an accepted treatment. They'll pay for medications because those are in the formulary. But supplements, dietary changes, functional medicine testing, these aren't covered. Not because they don't work. Because the system isn't set up to acknowledge them as valid treatments. This creates a financial barrier for most families. The interventions that might actually help are out of pocket. The interventions that just manage symptoms are covered.

All of these forces work together to suppress information and maintain the status quo. Nobody needs to be actively evil. Everyone is just operating within their incentive structures.

Dentists protecting their profession. Doctors practicing what they were taught. Pharmaceutical companies maximizing profits. Regulators maintaining relationships. Media companies keeping advertisers happy. Researchers seeking funding. Parents being told to trust the experts.

The system doesn't need a conspiracy to suppress truth. It just needs everyone doing what's rational within their local incentive structure. And because everyone is doing what's locally rational, the globally irrational outcome, sick kids and poisoned generations, continues. This is how systems fail without anyone being individually responsible. This is why change is so hard.

But understanding the incentive structures helps us understand why we're on our own. Nobody is coming to save us. The system can't acknowledge this problem without collapsing. So we build parallel systems. We share information peer to peer. We help each other's kids heal. We document results. And eventually, when enough people have undeniable evidence of recovery, the official story will have to change. But we can't wait for that. We start now, with what we know, helping who we can.

Chapter 13: The Bigger Picture

Now we get into the really uncomfortable territory. The stuff that sounds crazy until we look at the patterns. We can't prove intentionality here. But we can observe what happened and ask questions nobody wants us to ask.

About one hundred years ago, something changed in how society was organized. The early 1900s saw an explosion of industrial chemistry, pharmaceuticals developed from chemical warfare research, the creation of modern advertising and propaganda techniques, and the beginning of what we might call social engineering. This isn't conspiracy theory. This is documented history. The question is whether what happened next was accidental or planned.

World War I gave us chemical weapons. After the war, chemists who developed poison gas needed something to do with their knowledge and infrastructure. Many went into pharmaceutical development. The same chemical processes used to create mustard gas were applied to creating medications. This connection is documented. IG Farben, the German chemical conglomerate, produced both Zyklon B and early pharmaceuticals. These aren't separate industries. They're the same industry wearing different hats.

The 1920s and 30s saw the establishment of mandatory vaccination programs. Before this, vaccination was a choice. After this, increasingly required for school attendance, employment, military service. The infrastructure for injecting every child got built during this period. We're told this was purely for public health. Maybe it was. But it also created a system where every human could be dosed with whatever the authorities decided to put in those injections. The potential for control, whether used or not, became built into society.

Around the same time, 1930s and 40s, we see the beginning of water fluoridation. Officially for dental health, though the evidence for that has always been weak and the evidence for harm has been suppressed. Fluoride is a byproduct of aluminum and phosphate manufacturing. What do we do with toxic industrial waste? Convince people to put it in their drinking water. Again, maybe the motivation was genuinely health-oriented. Or maybe it was waste disposal with a PR campaign. And maybe the fact that fluoride makes people more docile, less likely to question authority, was a happy accident. Or, *maybe* it wasn't.

We see the widespread adoption of amalgam fillings despite early evidence of harm. Mercury, one of the most toxic substances known, installed permanently in people's mouths. Accumulating in the brain. Passed to children. Why would any sane medical system do this? Either incompetence or intention. Either they didn't know and didn't care to find out, or they knew and did it anyway. Neither answer is comforting.

Then something interesting happens around 1940 to 1960. We see a massive increase in pharmaceutical use, more vaccines added to the schedule, industrial chemicals in everything, processed food replacing real food, and the beginning of consumer culture and television. Each of these individually might be coincidence. Together they create a system where the population is increasingly controlled. Controlled biochemically through toxins and deficiency. Controlled psychologically through media and advertising. Controlled socially through medication and diagnosis.

By the 1960s and 70s, we start seeing the fruits of this. Drug culture explodes. Not organically, by the way. There's documented CIA involvement in LSD distribution, documented government involvement in heroin trafficking. The war on drugs gets declared right after the government floods communities with drugs. Create the problem, offer the solution, increase control. This is a documented pattern, not speculation. Soon we see the DARE program, where kids were taught about drugs and how people use them, almost like a training session.

The 1980s bring us the autism increase, ADHD diagnosis explosion, and the beginning of mass antidepressant use. Each generation more medicated than the last. Each generation more dependent on the system. Each generation less capable of functioning independently. Is this failure or success? Depends on who we ask. For pharmaceutical companies, it's wildly successful. For the population, it's a disaster. But nobody seems to be in charge of optimizing for population wellbeing.

Now look at where we are. One in thirty-six kids with autism. Anxiety and depression at record highs. Most adults on at least one medication. Attention spans destroyed. Critical thinking nearly extinct. A population that can barely function without constant pharmaceutical and technological intervention. And we're told this is just how things are. Modern life is stressful. Genetics, bad luck, mysterious. Nobody asks whether this was engineered.

Here's where it gets weird. Look at what autistic brains can do. Pattern recognition at superhuman levels. Ability to focus intensely on complex systems. Tolerance for repetitive tasks. Reduced social needs meaning less distraction from work. The tech industry runs on people with autistic traits. Silicon Valley is full of people on the spectrum. The computers and advanced technology we're increasingly dependent on were largely built by neurology that we call disordered.

So here's an uncomfortable question: what if autism isn't collateral damage? What if it's a feature? What if creating a subset of the population with altered neurology that excels at systematic thinking was part of the plan? We get enough high-functioning autistic people to build and maintain the technological control grid. We get enough low-functioning autistic people to create a permanent dependent class that justifies pharmaceutical intervention and government programs. We damage the middle enough that everyone needs medication to cope.

We can't prove this. But we can observe that if someone wanted to create a controlled, medicated, technologically dependent population, the system we have is exactly what they'd build. And we can observe that people with autistic traits are disproportionately involved in building the systems that control modern life. Technology, finance, advanced mathematics, all fields where autistic cognition excels and all fields that create mechanisms of control.

Look at what's coming. Artificial intelligence, brain-computer interfaces, genetic engineering, pharmaceutical genetic modification, digital currency, social credit systems. All of this requires the kind of systematic thinking that autistic neurology provides. All of this creates more control. All of this makes independent human function less possible. And all of this is being built largely by people whose neurology was altered by the same toxins we're discussing.

Mercury alters how brains develop. This is documented. It creates changes that, in some contexts, we call disability. In other contexts, we call genius. Ability to see patterns others can't see. Ability to work with complex abstract systems. Reduced emotional interference with logical processing. These are the traits we see in high-functioning autism. These are the traits we need to build and maintain technological civilization. Coincidence?

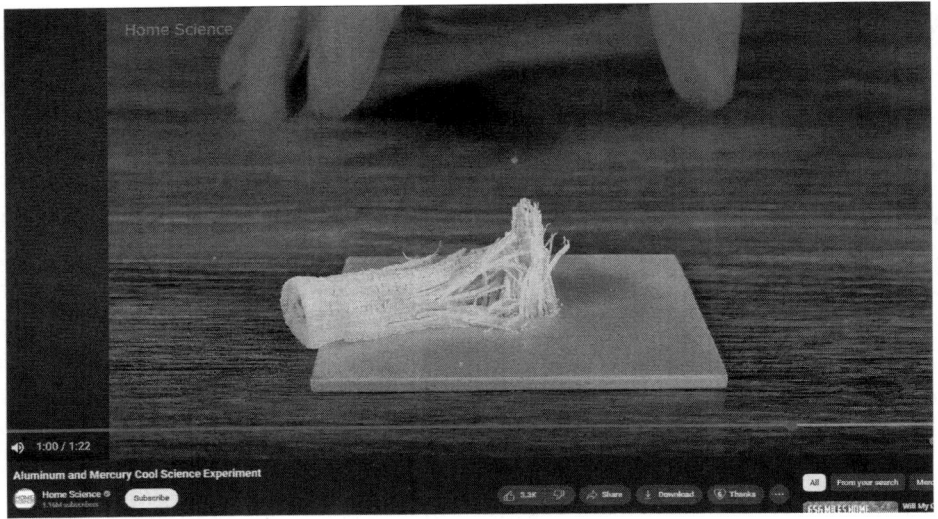

This YouTube screenshot is showing what happens when mercury and aluminum are combined. Over time they form these odd filaments that extend. I suspect this is happening in microscopic ways in our neurons and causing things to connect where they should not connect. If this happens during development, things are likely locked into place. If this starts happening after development, or the stress becomes worse, we can likely reverse that with proper nutritient balancing.

The human brain evolved for a low-tech environment. Social connection, pattern recognition in nature, physical problem solving. The modern world requires different cognition. Abstract systematic thinking, tolerance for artificial environments, comfort with technology. Maybe mercury exposure is accidentally creating the neurology required for the world we're building. Or maybe someone figured this out and accelerated the process. We can't know. But we can observe the correlation.

Here's another uncomfortable observation. The same families who pushed industrial mercury, pharmaceutical expansion, water fluoridation, and mass vaccination are the families who became incredibly wealthy and powerful. This isn't conspiracy theory. This is public record. We can trace the money. We can see who benefited. And we can ask whether that benefit was accidental or intended. The answer might be both. Systems can be opportunistic without being planned. But at some point, coincidence strains credibility.

What do we do with this information? We can't prove intentionality. We probably never will. The people with answers aren't talking and the evidence that might exist isn't accessible. But we don't need to prove intentionality to act. We can see what's happening to our bodies and our kids' bodies. We can see what works to fix it. And we can help each other do that, regardless of whether the damage was accidental or planned.

Maybe this is all coincidence. Maybe industrial society just happened to poison itself in ways that accidentally created useful neurological variants while making everyone dependent on pharmaceutical intervention. Maybe the people who profited weren't aware of what they were doing. Maybe every step was innocent and we're just seeing patterns where none exist.

Or maybe this was the largest biochemical social engineering experiment in human history. Maybe creating an autism epidemic was the price of creating technological civilization. Maybe our kids are collateral damage in a transition nobody asked if we wanted. Maybe we're living through something so big and so dark that most people can't look at it directly.

We don't need to know which is true to know what we need to do. Get the poison out. Rebuild the system. Help our kids function. Build parallel networks of people who understand. And ask questions that make powerful people uncomfortable. Because whether this is conspiracy or coincidence, the outcome is the same. We're being poisoned, our kids are being damaged, and the system that did it isn't going to fix it.

We're on our own. Time to act like it.

Keep in mind. No matter what is happening, this is human nature. This is what we eventually do. We keep organizing stuff to move forward in some way.

Or, maybe humans aren't the ones steering the ship..

Chapter 14: What Now?

So we're at the end. We understand the mechanism. We understand why it's suppressed. We understand the scale of what we're dealing with. Now what?

First, accept that we're building parallel systems. The mainstream medical system isn't going to help with this. They can't, even if some of them wanted to. The incentive structures won't allow it. So we build our own networks. Parent groups, online communities, practitioners who understand functional medicine. We share information peer to peer. We document what works. We help each other navigate this.

This means becoming our own experts. Reading research. Learning biochemistry. Understanding our own bodies and our kids' bodies better than any doctor who sees us for fifteen minutes. This isn't ideal, but it's reality. We're the ones who care most about our own health and our kids' health. We're the ones who'll put in the time to figure this out. We become the experts by necessity.

Find our people. There are communities of parents doing this work. There are practitioners, though they're often operating on the fringes and many have been attacked or had licenses threatened. There are researchers who couldn't get funding through official channels but kept investigating anyway. These people exist. They're harder to find because they're suppressed, but they're out there. Connect with them. Learn from them. Build relationships. We need each other. I've started a page of links that I've been able to quickly research pathwaymap.com/autism-links and I plan on adding a form in case you'd like to add any.

Start with the basics and don't get overwhelmed. Sunlight, real food, reduce toxins, support the drain. These are simple things that cost little and carry low risk. We don't need to have the perfect protocol figured out on day one. We just need to start moving in the right direction. Small consistent changes compound over time. Focus on what we can control. Let go of what we can't.

Document everything. Keep a simple log of what we're doing and what we're observing. Dates, supplements added or removed, dosages, behavioral observations, sleep quality, gut function. Over time, patterns will emerge. We'll see what helps and what doesn't. This becomes our personal research. This is how we figure out what our specific bodies need. One size does not fit all. Our journal tells us what fits us.

Be patient with the process and with ourselves. This takes time. Years, not weeks. We're undoing damage that accumulated over generations. We're rebuilding systems that have been broken our whole lives. Some days will feel like progress. Some days will feel like regression. Both are part of the process. Keep showing up. Keep supporting the system. Trust that the body wants to heal and will heal when we remove obstacles and provide support.

Protect our energy and our boundaries. This work is demanding. We're swimming against the current. We're going against medical advice. We're being told we're harming our kids by people who don't understand. This takes a toll. We need to protect ourselves. Limit time with people who undermine us. Limit exposure to media that makes us doubt ourselves. Find communities that support what we're doing. We can't pour from an empty cup.

Forgive ourselves for not knowing sooner. Many of us are doing this work after our kids have already suffered for years. After we've already suffered for years. We might feel guilt or anger at ourselves for not figuring this out earlier. Let it go. We didn't know because the information was suppressed. We're doing our best with what we have now. That's enough. Keep moving forward. Be grateful you are aware, and not just digging deeper.

Share what we learn, but choose our audience carefully. Not everyone is ready to hear this. Not everyone wants to know. Some people need to believe the system is working and will get hostile if we challenge that belief. We can't help people who don't want help. Focus on the people who are ready, who are asking questions, who sense something is wrong and are looking for answers. Those are our people. Help them. Let the others be. Lead by example so they want to know what we're up to.

Try to formulate your words and messages in a way that allows you to send them off on their own. Allow people to take them in, or not. But do not remain attached to them. Do what you can and move on, if someone bites, repeat. Lead by example. An awesome example.

Vote with your dollars where possible. Buy from companies that aren't poisoning us. Support practitioners who understand this approach. Buy supplements from companies that prioritize quality. Avoid products with seed oils, excess sugar, artificial ingredients. Each dollar is a vote for the kind of world we want. We can't avoid the system entirely, but we can minimize how much we fund it.

Prepare for resistance and gaslighting. Family members will tell us we're being ridiculous. Doctors will tell us we're endangering our kids. Online communities will call us anti-science. Schools will push back on dietary accommodations. Insurance won't cover anything. This is normal. This is what happens when we go against the system. Expect it. Don't let it derail us. We know what we've observed. We know what's working. Stay the course.

When someone says something dumb and you feel the urge to get annoyed, think of someone you know who says dumb stuff and who never seems to know what's going on. Find a way to 'look down' on the person, because when we break it down, that's how it should be. Normal people have normal conversations, not ones based on combating marketing or media talking points.

Build skills that make us less dependent. Learn to cook real food. Learn to grow some food if possible. Learn about herbs and natural remedies. Learn to read research papers and evaluate evidence. Learn about water filtration, EMF reduction, detox protocols. Each skill makes us more resilient. Each skill means we need the system less. This is how we create real independence.

Think about community resilience, not just individual health. Connect with neighbors. Build relationships with local farmers. Support local practitioners. Create networks of people who understand. When the system fails, and it will continue failing, we'll need each other. Start building those connections now. Community is the ultimate safety net.

Teach our kids what we're learning, in age-appropriate ways. Help them understand their bodies. Help them make connections between what they eat and how they feel. Give them tools to take care of themselves. This isn't about making them paranoid. It's about giving them literacy about their own bodies that most people never get. These are life skills that will serve them forever.

Consider the next generation. If we're healing ourselves, if we're helping our kids heal, they'll have a better baseline when they have their own kids. Each generation can be stronger than the last if we break the cycle. This is how we reverse the damage. One family at a time, one generation at a time, rebuilding what was broken. We might not see the full fruits in our lifetime. But our grandkids might. That's worth working for.

Stay humble about what we know and don't know. We're figuring this out as we go. What works for one person might not work for another. What we think is true today might be refined tomorrow. Hold our theories lightly. Hold our observations seriously. Be willing to adjust as we learn more. Dogma is the enemy of understanding. Stay curious. Stay flexible.

Find meaning in the struggle. This is hard. But it's also purposeful. We're not just victims of a broken system. We're pioneers figuring out how to heal from something the official world won't acknowledge. We're building knowledge that could help thousands of other families. We're proving that recovery is possible. That's meaningful. That matters. When the days are hard, remember why we're doing this.

Celebrate the wins, no matter how small. First full night of sleep in months. First time our kid made eye contact unprompted. First day without a meltdown. First food reintroduced successfully. These aren't small things. These are miracles. Each one proves the system is healing. Each one proves this approach works. Acknowledge them. Let ourselves feel the progress. This is how we sustain ourselves for the long haul.

Accept that we might never have all the answers. We might never know if this was intentional or accidental. We might never get official acknowledgment or apology. We might never see the people responsible held accountable. That's okay. We're not doing this for validation or justice. We're doing this because our kids need help and we're the ones who can provide it. Focus on what we can control. Let go of what we can't.

Build something better. As we heal, as our kids heal, as we connect with others doing this work, we're creating a new way. A way that prioritizes health over profit. A way that empowers individuals instead of creating dependence. A way that seeks root causes instead of managing symptoms. This is the world we want. We create it by living it. One family at a time. One decision at a time. One healed kid at a time.

The system isn't going to fix this. But we don't need the system to fix it. We have each other. We have the information. We have the tools. We have the motivation. That's enough. We start where we are. We do what we can. We help who we can help. And we trust that as more people wake up, as more kids heal, as more families find their way out of this nightmare, the official story will have to change. But we don't wait for that. We act now.

Our kids are counting on us. Our own bodies are counting on us. Future generations are counting on us. This is our responsibility and our opportunity. Nobody is coming to save us. We save ourselves. We save each other. We build the world we want to live in. And we do it whether the system approves or not.

This is how we win. Not by waiting for permission. Not by playing by rules designed to keep us sick. Not by hoping the people who broke us will fix us. We win by understanding what happened, addressing it systematically, helping each other through the process, and building parallel systems that actually work. We win by refusing to accept that our kids' struggles are permanent. We win by proving recovery is possible. We win by being undeniable.

The drain was clogged. We're unclogging it. One family at a time. Together. Let's get to work.

Epilogue: A Note to Parents

If we're reading this as parents of autistic children, we're probably exhausted. We've been fighting for years. Fighting for diagnoses, fighting for services, fighting for understanding, fighting for our kids to be seen and helped. And maybe we've been fighting ourselves too, wondering what we did wrong, what we could have done differently.

Here's what we need to know: we didn't cause this. Our kids didn't cause this. This was done to all of us by systems that prioritized profit over people, that prioritized convenience over health, that prioritized control over truth. We're all victims here. All of us trying to survive in a world that was engineered to break us.

But here's the other thing we need to know: recovery is possible. Not always complete. Not always easy. But possible. We've seen it. Kids who couldn't speak, speaking. Kids who couldn't connect, connecting. Kids who couldn't tolerate food, eating normally. Adults dependant on care, living their own lives. It happens. More often than we're told. The stories don't get shared widely because they threaten too many interests. But they exist.

Our kids are not broken. Their systems are jammed. There's a difference. Broken means unfixable. Jammed means stuck with obstacles. We can remove obstacles. We can unjam systems. We can support the body's natural drive to heal. And when we do, function improves. Sometimes dramatically. Sometimes slowly. But it improves.

This isn't false hope. This is documented, reproducible results that get ignored because they're inconvenient. This is biochemistry, not magic. This is understanding mechanism and addressing root cause instead of just managing symptoms. This works. Not for everyone identically. Not overnight. But it works.

We're going to feel alone in this sometimes. Doctors will tell us we're wrong. Family will tell us we're making it worse. Schools will resist. Insurance won't help. Online communities will attack us. This is normal. This is what happens when we challenge systems that profit from keeping us sick. Expect resistance. Don't let it stop us.

Find our people. They're out there. Parents who've walked this path. Practitioners who understand. Communities that support recovery instead of just acceptance. These people will sustain us when it gets hard. And it will get hard. This is years of work. But we're not alone in it.

Start simple. Sunlight, real food, reduce obvious toxins. These are things we can do tomorrow that carry almost no risk and cost very little. We don't need the perfect protocol. We don't need expensive testing. We don't need permission from doctors. We just need to start supporting our kids' bodies and removing obstacles. The body does the rest.

Document what we observe. Not for anyone else. For ourselves. So we can see the patterns. So we can see the progress even when it feels like nothing is changing. So we have evidence when we start to doubt. Keep it simple. Dates, changes, observations. That's enough.

Be patient. With the process. With our kids. With ourselves. This didn't happen overnight and it won't fix overnight. Some days will be hard. Some days we'll want to give up. That's normal. Keep going anyway. Every small step forward is progress. Every day we're supporting the system is a day closer to healing.

Forgive ourselves for the times we fed them things that made them worse because we didn't know. For the times we followed doctor's orders that didn't help. For the times we were impatient or frustrated or couldn't understand why they were struggling. We were doing our best with broken information in a broken system. We're doing better now. That's what matters.

Celebrate every win. The first time they sleep through the night. The first food they tolerate. The first time they look at us and we know they're really seeing us. These matter. These are everything. Don't let the hard days make us forget the progress. Keep track of wins. Return to them when we need hope.

Know that our kids feel our stress. They're affected by our emotional state. This is biochemical, not just psychological. When we're in fight-or-flight, they feel it. When we're at peace, they feel that too. Taking care of ourselves isn't selfish. It's necessary. We can't pour from an empty cup. Our healing supports their healing. This is a family process.

Trust our instincts. We know our kids better than any professional who sees them for an hour. If something feels wrong, it probably is. If we see improvement with an intervention, we're probably right even if doctors say we're imagining it. We're the experts on our own kids. Act like it. We have permission to trust what we observe.

Remember why we're doing this. Not to make our kids "normal." Not to make them easier to manage. Not to make them fit into a broken system. We're doing this so they can think clearly. So they can feel comfortable in their bodies. So they can connect with the world without constant overwhelm. So they can reach their potential, whatever that is for them. We're removing obstacles. What they build with that is up to them.

Our kids are not less than. They're not broken. They're not mistakes. They're humans with jammed metabolic systems trying to function in a toxic world. We're helping them unjam those systems. As we do, their true selves can emerge. That self was always there. It was just buried under biochemical chaos. We're clearing the chaos. We're revealing who they actually are.

This is hard work. Probably the hardest thing we'll ever do. But it's also the most important. We're not just helping our kids. We're breaking a generational cycle. We're proving recovery is possible. We're building knowledge and community that will help countless other families. We're changing the paradigm one healed kid at a time.

We can do this. We're already doing this. Every day we show up for our kids, we're doing it. Every meal we prepare with care. Every supplement we plan. Every time we choose real food over processed. Every time we get them outside in the sun. Every time we stay calm when they're melting down. Every time we advocate when they need help. We're doing it.

Our kids are lucky to have us. Parents who won't accept that this struggle is permanent. Parents who'll question authority when it's not helping. Parents who'll swim against the current to find what actually works. Parents who love them enough to do years of hard work with no guarantee of outcomes. That's not nothing. That's everything.

Keep going. One day at a time. One step at a time. One small improvement at a time. This path leads somewhere better. We might not be able to see it from here. But it does. Trust the process. Trust our observations. Trust that the body wants to heal and will heal when we give it what it needs and remove what's in the way.

We've got this. Together. Thanks for being part of it.

Read my other free ebooks about digestion, MTHFR, and iodine at pathwaymap.com/books and follow me on Facebook facebook.com/micah.john.coffey and YouTube youtube.com/sickoftired

Maybe one day I'll find the words to express what I've managed to stumble on. Till then I invite you to explore what I have created. I've created and shared a ton of free content over the years.

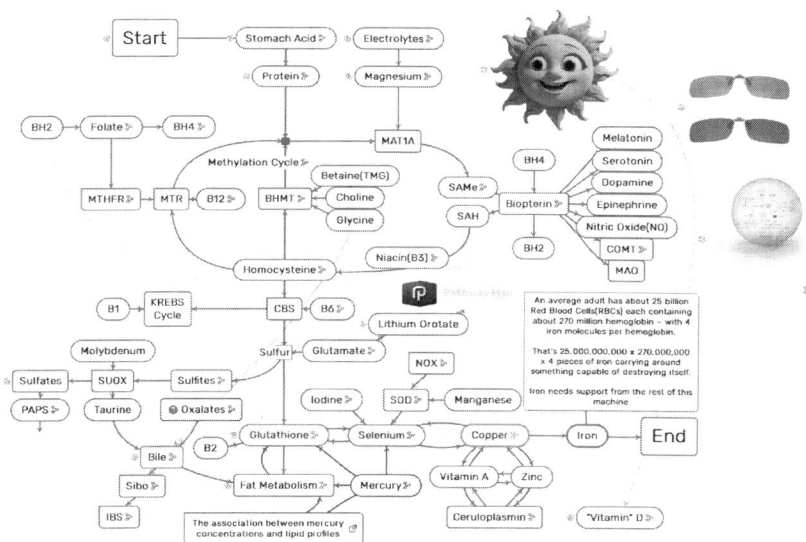

This screenshot is part of an interactive mindmap that can be downloaded from pathwaymap.com. It depends on an app that may or may not be free depending on the device you are using. If you find this type of info and method of organization, this is an incredible way to learn more about how these things work together. My interactive map has over 2,000 datapoints which all essentially branch off of this screenshot.

I create these things in my free time, which means they are not always complete, not always organized well, and they do not always advertise their potential.

I am slowly gaining support which will allow me to make my resources look a bit more like we might expect. Till then you have to search a bit or ask me in order to find all the things

Printed in Dunstable, United Kingdom